Jeffrey Finds His Way

Written by

Tammy Vallieres MacRae and Susan Lucente-Rizzo

Illustration and Design by

Jerrold Hewson

Balboa Press books may be ordered through booksellers or by contacting:

Balboa Press
A Division of Hay House
1663 Liberty Drive
Bloomington, IN 47403
www.balboapress.com
1-(877) 407-4847

Because of the dynamic nature of the Internet, any web addresses or links contained in this book may have changed since publication and may no longer be valid. The views expressed in this work are solely those of the author and do not necessarily reflect the views of the publisher, and the publisher hereby disclaims any responsibility for them.

The author of this book does not dispense medical advice or prescribe the use of any technique as a form of treatment for physical, emotional, or medical problems without the advice of a physician, either directly or indirectly. The intent of the author is only to offer information of a general nature to help you in your quest for emotional and spiritual well-being. In the event you use any of the information in this book for yourself, which is your constitutional right, the author and the publisher assume no responsibility for your actions.

Any people depicted in stock imagery provided by Thinkstock are models, and such images are being used for illustrative purposes only.

Certain stock imagery © Thinkstock.

Printed in the United States of America

Balboa Press rev. date:5/1/2012

BALBOA
PRESS
A DIVISION OF HAY HOUSE

From the top of the pearly gates Jeffrey stared past the clouds, puzzled that a small planet could cause him such pain. "Why does it make my heart ache?" Jeffery sighed.

"Little angel," said a voice from below, "you have within you the power that lets you see what others cannot. Don't be frightened. Let it guide you."

"What do you mean?" Jeffrey asked.

God smiled up at Jeffrey and continued on his way.

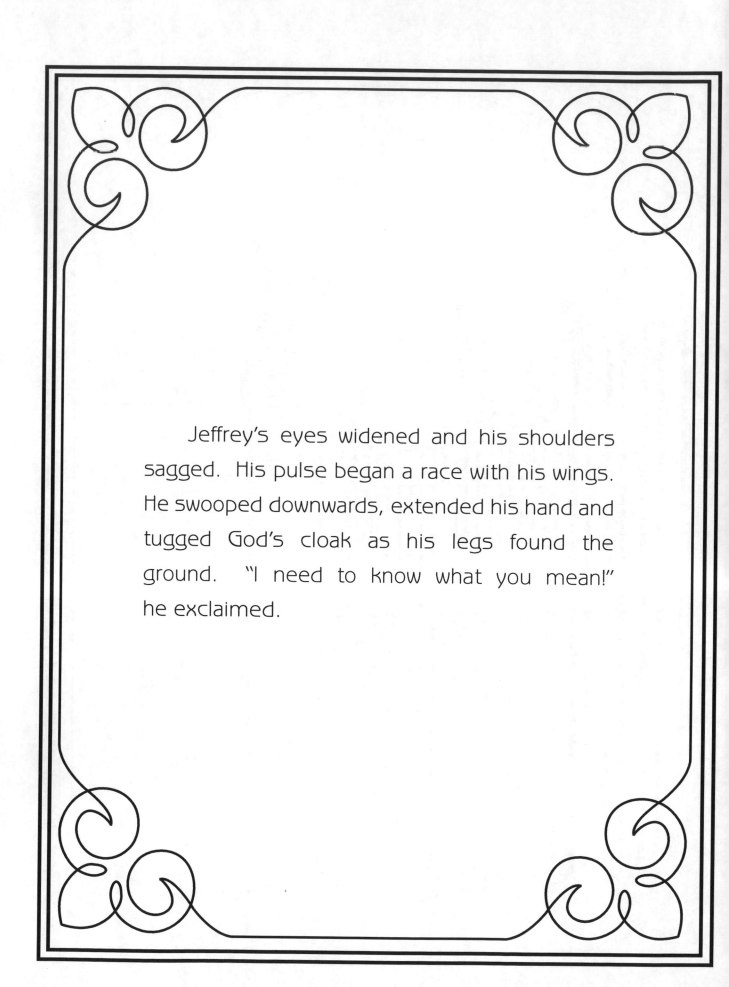

Jeffrey's eyes widened and his shoulders sagged. His pulse began a race with his wings. He swooped downwards, extended his hand and tugged God's cloak as his legs found the ground. "I need to know what you mean!" he exclaimed.

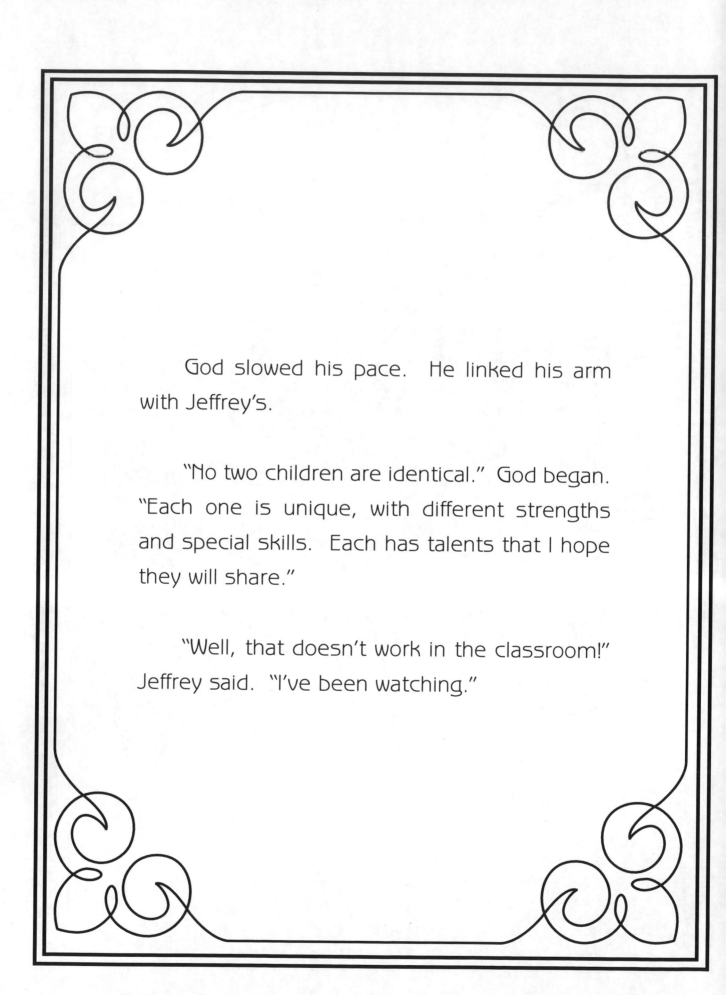

God slowed his pace. He linked his arm with Jeffrey's.

"No two children are identical." God began. "Each one is unique, with different strengths and special skills. Each has talents that I hope they will share."

"Well, that doesn't work in the classroom!" Jeffrey said. "I've been watching."

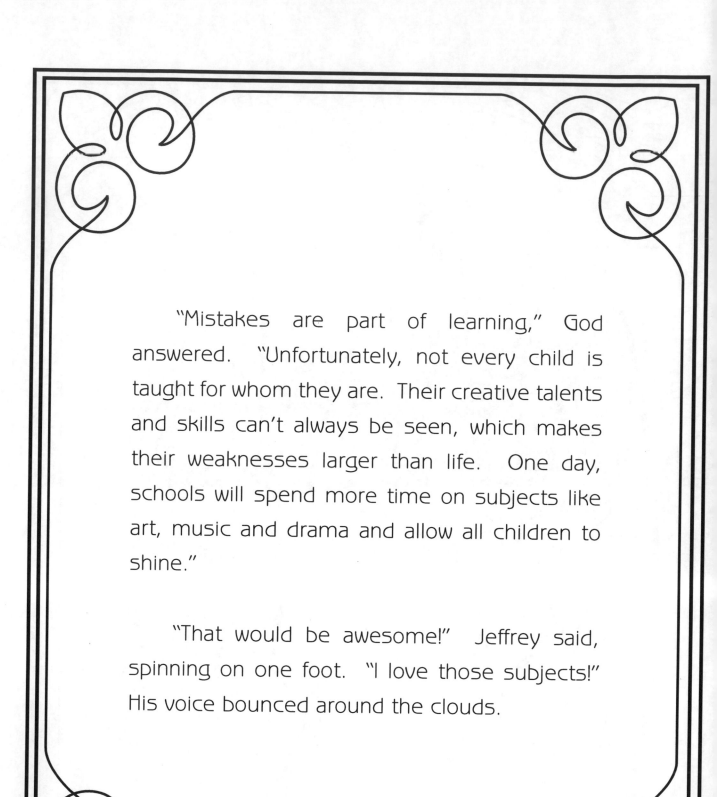

"Mistakes are part of learning," God answered. "Unfortunately, not every child is taught for whom they are. Their creative talents and skills can't always be seen, which makes their weaknesses larger than life. One day, schools will spend more time on subjects like art, music and drama and allow all children to shine."

"That would be awesome!" Jeffrey said, spinning on one foot. "I love those subjects!" His voice bounced around the clouds.

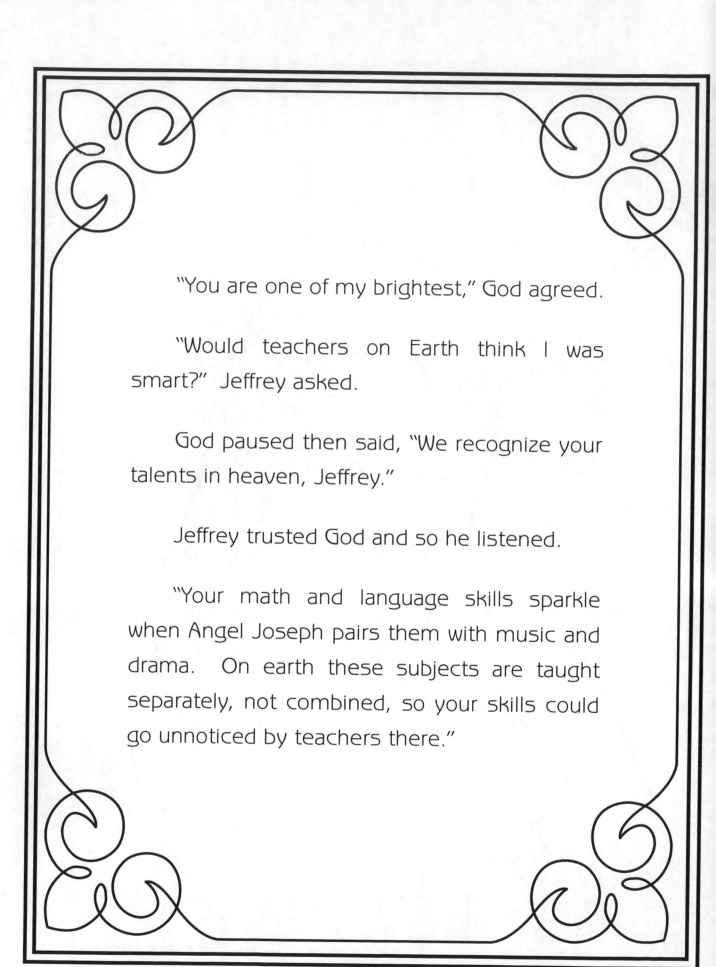

"You are one of my brightest," God agreed.

"Would teachers on Earth think I was smart?" Jeffrey asked.

God paused then said, "We recognize your talents in heaven, Jeffrey."

Jeffrey trusted God and so he listened.

"Your math and language skills sparkle when Angel Joseph pairs them with music and drama. On earth these subjects are taught separately, not combined, so your skills could go unnoticed by teachers there."

"You blessed me with powers to see what others cannot." "Well…" Jeffrey's lips quivered. "Take them back if I can't use them!"

"Special gifts are not returnable," God said. "Your job is to find the best way to use them."

"But what good are my powers here in heaven?" Jeffrey's voice soared above the clouds. "And why don't you show earth's children how to shine?"

"Slow down, little soul. One question at a time."

Jeffrey paused. "If I can see what others cannot..." He took a deep breath. "God, I must travel to earth. I must show them what needs to be done! Please!" he begged. "I can help these children understand their special gifts, and teach them how to use them. Maybe I can convince teachers to make more time for the important subjects."

"Now, Jeffrey," God chuckled, "all subjects are equally important and valuable."

"I'm sorry... I couldn't help myself!" Jeffrey confessed with a grin.

"My precious son," God said. "Are you sure you're ready for this?"

"You gave me these powers for a reason," Jeffrey answered with a firm nod. "Now I must use them!" His heart raced with excitement, and the twinkle in his eyes matched the stars.

"I will agree to your request on one condition - that an angel who is your exact opposite travels with you for support."

"Is that all?" Jeffrey pushed his hair out of his eyes. "No problem!" His wings began to flap. He flung his halo into the air. "Thanks, God! I'm going right now!" Then he soared like an eagle to find his perfect match.

Jeffrey was an excellent artist, and he had a flare with his pen. He was also shy around people, especially adults. His opposite would be skilled in computers, math and science and have oodles of self-confidence.

Jeffrey landed with a thump inches from the pearly gates. He sat with his cloak draped over his head and began to giggle. Then he stood up and walked towards Emanuel, an angel who knew more about numbers than anyone else: he kept track of everyone in heaven. Jeffrey's enthusiasm quickly swayed the other angel and they shook hands to seal the deal.

"We'll each choose a family," Jeffrey began. "There we'll grow and experience life's ups and downs."

"And teach them about compassion and empathy!" Emanuel added.

"Exactly," Jeffrey's joy was contagious. "So that all will understand and accept each other's differences."

They worked as a team, using their strengths to create the perfect plan. "Earth, here we come!" Jeffrey announced.

On departure day, God shed a tiny tear and reminded them to pray daily. Through their prayers they would receive God's guidance and support and never feel alone. He knew their task would be difficult, but his belief in their abilities was stronger.

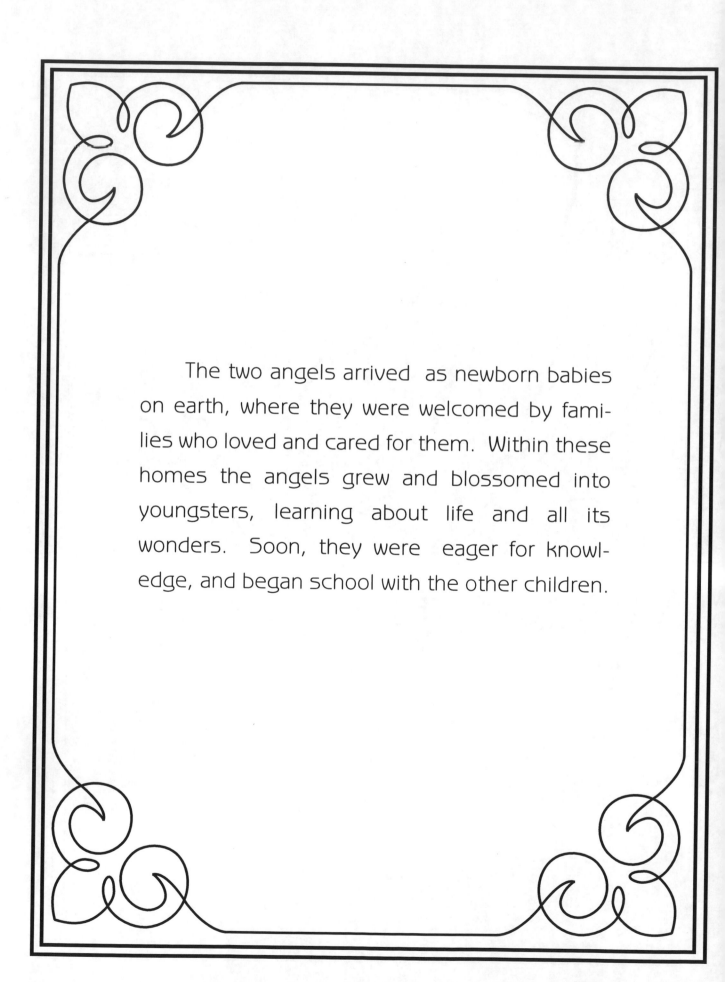

The two angels arrived as newborn babies on earth, where they were welcomed by families who loved and cared for them. Within these homes the angels grew and blossomed into youngsters, learning about life and all its wonders. Soon, they were eager for knowledge, and began school with the other children.

All was well until Grade 3, when Jeffrey began to feel different. By Grade 5, school seemed more like torture than learning.

"Jeffrey, you must concentrate." Mrs. Lee would often tell him, causing giggles to echo throughout the room.

When the sweet sound of the final bell roared through the halls, Jeffrey was finally free – though freedom lasted only as long as the walk home. Then came the 1000 questions. Nobody seemed to understand, not even when he explained…

"Mom, I try to **focus**, I really do, but the letters on the page **jump** around more than I do. I let my mind wander to stop the letters from **bouncing** so my head won't **explode**!"

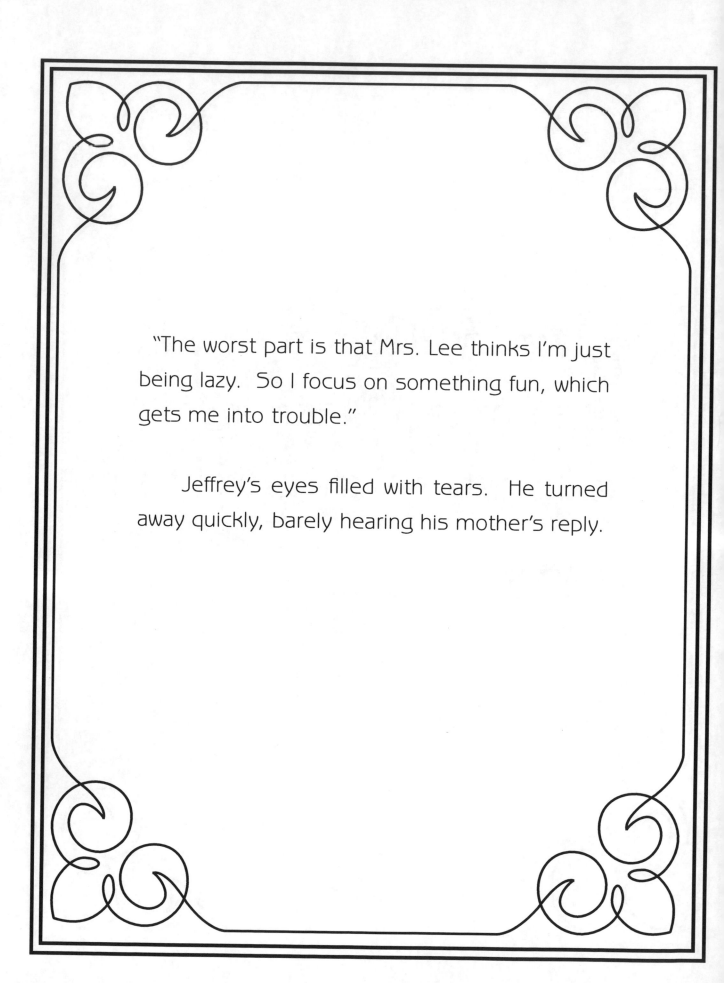

"The worst part is that Mrs. Lee thinks I'm just being lazy. So I focus on something fun, which gets me into trouble."

Jeffrey's eyes filled with tears. He turned away quickly, barely hearing his mother's reply.

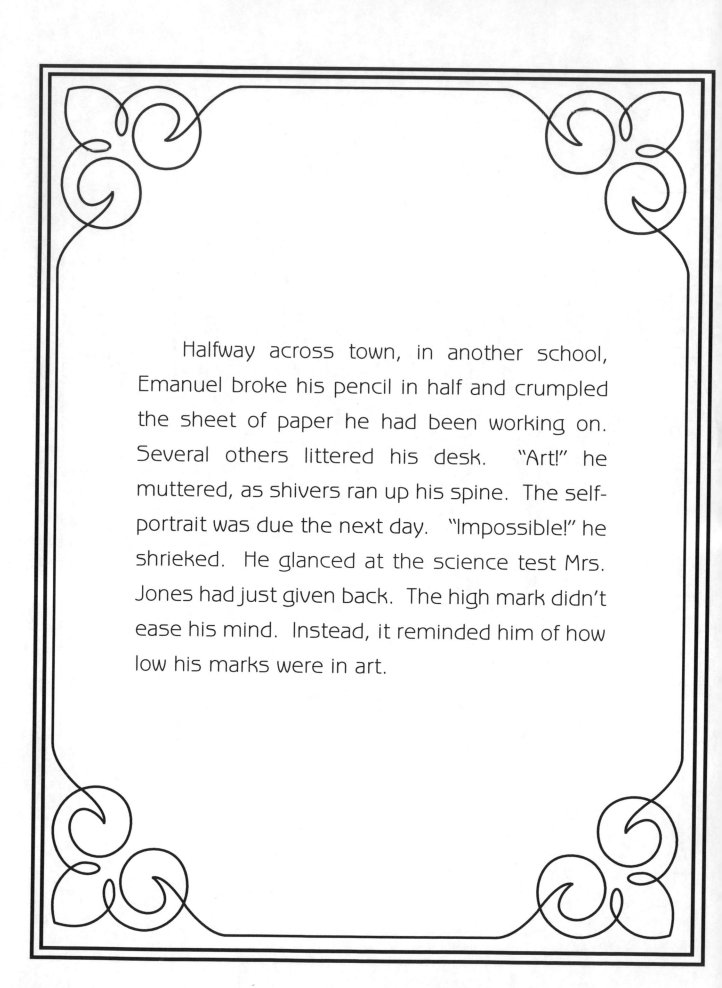

Halfway across town, in another school, Emanuel broke his pencil in half and crumpled the sheet of paper he had been working on. Several others littered his desk. "Art!" he muttered, as shivers ran up his spine. The self-portrait was due the next day. "Impossible!" he shrieked. He glanced at the science test Mrs. Jones had just given back. The high mark didn't ease his mind. Instead, it reminded him of how low his marks were in art.

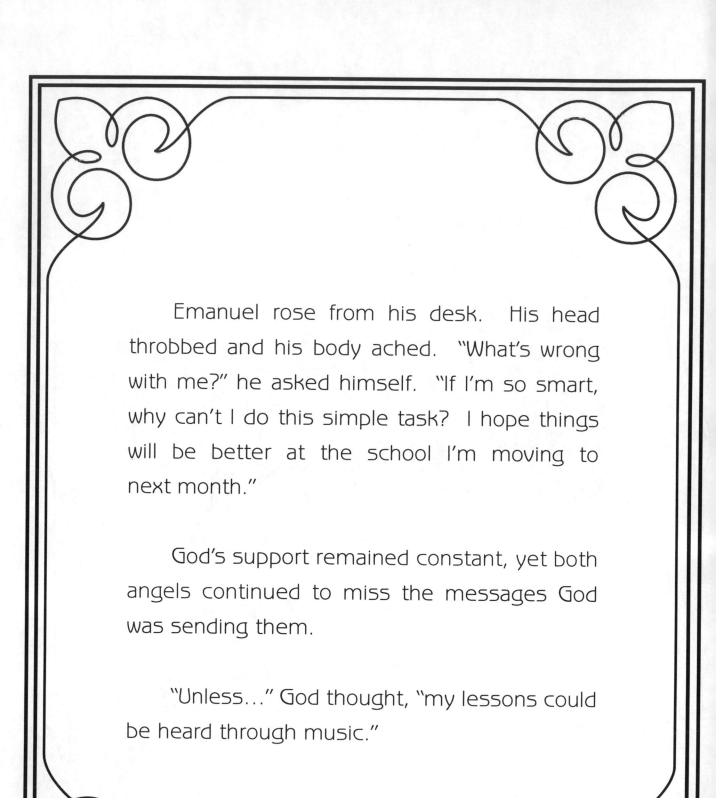

Emanuel rose from his desk. His head throbbed and his body ached. "What's wrong with me?" he asked himself. "If I'm so smart, why can't I do this simple task? I hope things will be better at the school I'm moving to next month."

God's support remained constant, yet both angels continued to miss the messages God was sending them.

"Unless..." God thought, "my lessons could be heard through music."

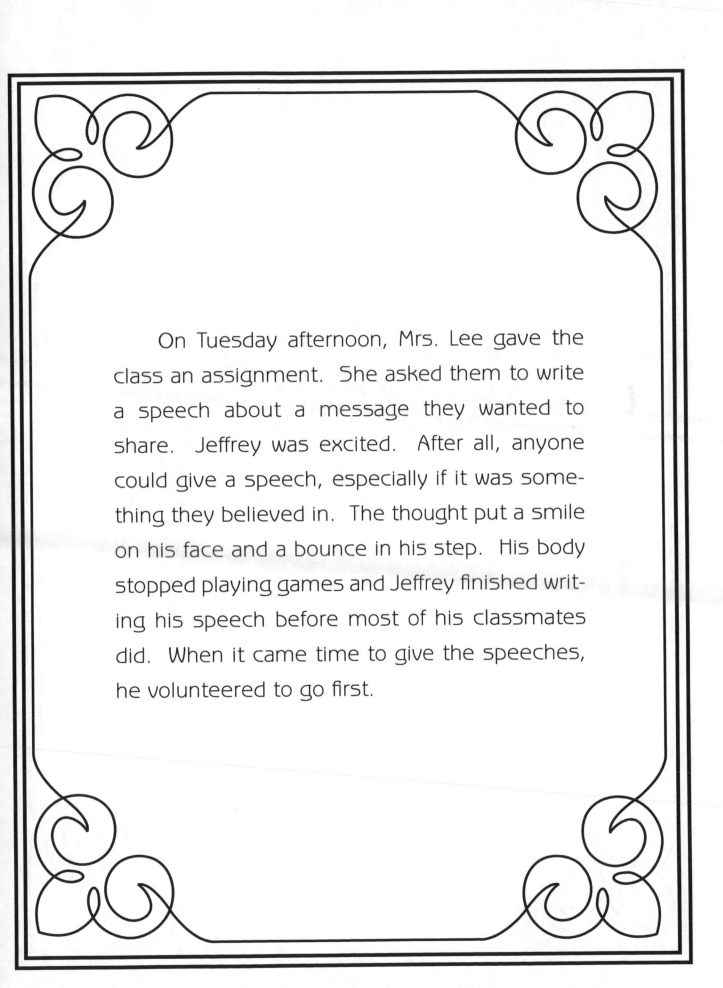

On Tuesday afternoon, Mrs. Lee gave the class an assignment. She asked them to write a speech about a message they wanted to share. Jeffrey was excited. After all, anyone could give a speech, especially if it was something they believed in. The thought put a smile on his face and a bounce in his step. His body stopped playing games and Jeffrey finished writing his speech before most of his classmates did. When it came time to give the speeches, he volunteered to go first.

"The title of my speech is 'We Have the Power'," Jeffrey said. He stood tall and smiled. He faced his classmates and drew them in with his eyes. He was calm and focused – the opposite of what they expected from him.

"Hold this thought," he said. "Creating Heaven, Here on Earth."

His words lingered and held everyone's attention.

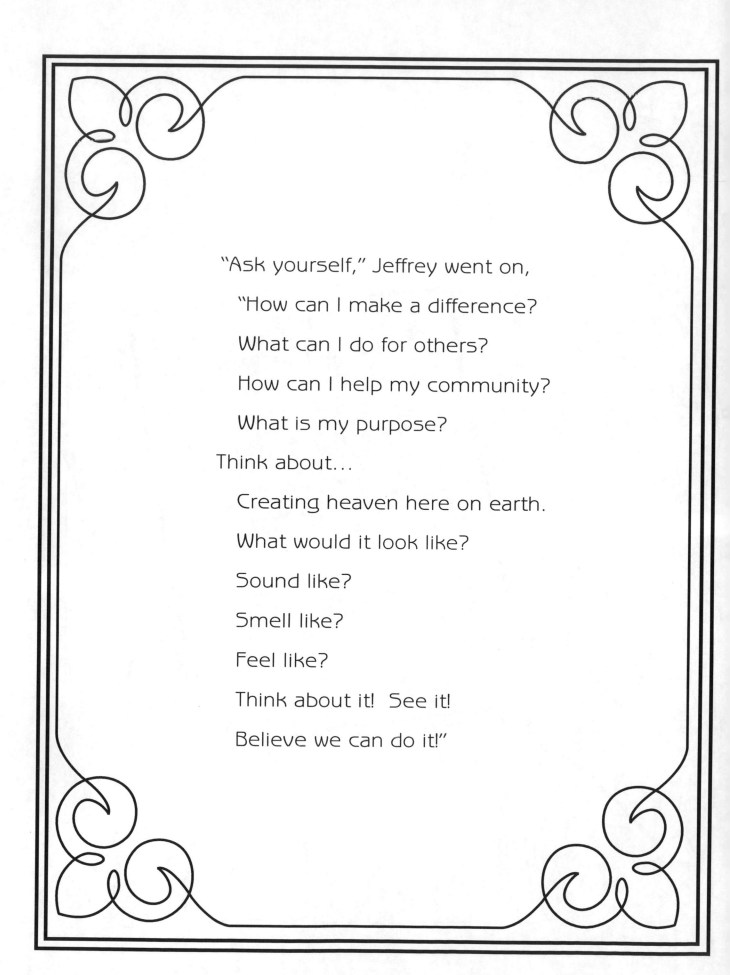

"Ask yourself," Jeffrey went on,

"How can I make a difference?

What can I do for others?

How can I help my community?

What is my purpose?

Think about...

Creating heaven here on earth.

What would it look like?

Sound like?

Smell like?

Feel like?

Think about it! See it!

Believe we can do it!"

Jeffrey's passion shone and his voice rose
to new heights.

"One step at a time, we could build this!"

He stepped closer to the other children.

"All of us are able to…

Learn from each other

Work as a team

Care for others

Build new things together

Protect our space

Respect differences

And SHINE BRIGHTLY!"

Jeffrey's hand shot towards the ceiling and his fingers danced. His spirit had come alive.

"Remember the story Mrs. Lee read to us about the strength of five branches compared to one?"

His eyes scanned the room. His classmates were nodding. Some smiled.

"Just think… if we put our gifts together, we too could be powerful!"

Jeffrey's arm became a sword. He winked and pointed to Sara to begin the song.

"Thank you," he concluded.

For a moment, all was silent, then Jeffrey spotted the new student sitting in the desk next to his. Their eyes met as everyone in the class clapped for Jeffrey. The new boy clapped, too.

"Wow, great speech!" the boy whispered as the next student began. "You must be the brains in this class. My name is Emanuel. What's yours?"

Jeffrey blushed. In a tiny voice he replied, "Thanks. I'm Jeffrey." A beam of sunlight from the window surrounded them.

The two boys became inseparable. Because each one had different gifts and talents, they could help each other learn. "A match made in heaven!" they joked of their friendship. "We're the ultimate team," they would say when their talents and skills were combined. "A dynamic duo! The A team!"

At his old arts school, Emanuel had felt lost and stupid. At his new school, he felt good about himself. He wondered. "Why is everything different when I haven't changed?" This puzzled him, especially since Jeffrey hated this school.

"I've got it!" Emanuel shouted. "It's the school's vision that is different, not me! My old school based everything around the arts, but here students are taught to earn high marks in other subjects. Art and drama are just for fun. No wonder Jeffrey feels lost."

Our School's Vision

That evening Emanuel knelt beside his bed and prayed. "God," he began, "I know we haven't spoken in a while, but I really need your help." His eyes fluttered shut as he shared everything he knew about his old school. Then he explained why it would be perfect for Jeffrey. He described the differences between the two schools and what he believed they were doing wrong. Then he mentioned how helpless he felt talking about this with Jeffrey.

"So, God," he whispered, "what should I do?" Then Emanuel crawled into bed, fully expecting an answer in the morning. Before his eyes closed he whispered, "Oh! And God, I promise to pray every night from now on, too. Amen."

Emanuel woke before dawn. "I'm ready, God, whenever you are..." He waited in the silence and darkness. When nothing happened, he announced, "God, patience is not one of my strengths." He chuckled as the clock beside his bed flashed: 5:55 a.m. He drummed his fingers on the pillow, "Jeffrey is smart!" he thought. "So why doesn't anyone, not even Jeffrey, acknowledge this fact? After all, he wrote and delivered a speech with more power and purpose than anyone else. Where did Jeffrey's spark go?"

"Any time, God!" he said as the sun rose, filling his room with a stream of bright, shiny beams of light.

"Of course," he whispered, sprinting from his bed towards the window. He gazed at the sky and addressed God. "The answer is in Jeffrey's speech! Right?" Emanuel's heart skipped a beat. "Jeffrey told everyone what needs to be done but no one, not even Jeffrey, listened to the words. Especially these ones: Respect Differences and Shine Brightly!"

For what seemed like forever Emanuel stood there. "Why were certain subjects ranked higher than the rest?" he wondered. "And why did no one notice how this affected a child's feelings?" "Even Mrs. Lee didn't understand how Jeffrey's struggles affected more than just good grades."

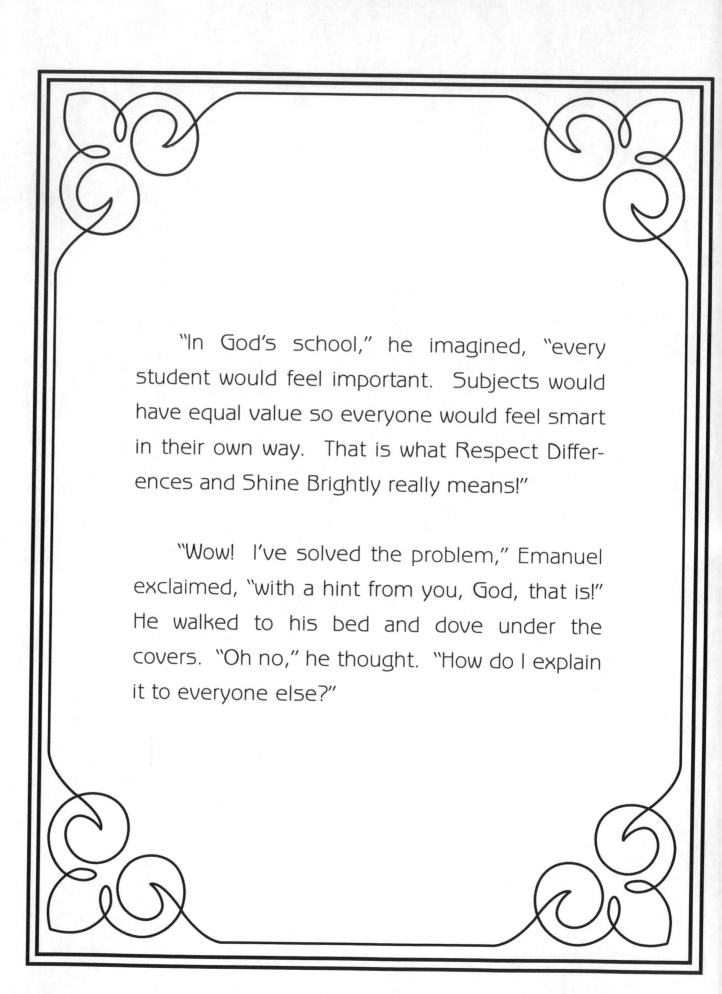

"In God's school," he imagined, "every student would feel important. Subjects would have equal value so everyone would feel smart in their own way. That is what Respect Differences and Shine Brightly really means!"

"Wow! I've solved the problem," Emanuel exclaimed, "with a hint from you, God, that is!" He walked to his bed and dove under the covers. "Oh no," he thought. "How do I explain it to everyone else?"

That day Emanuel arrived at school early. He needed to see Jeffrey's speech, which Mrs. Lee had hung on the back wall of their classroom.

"I'll start with Jeffrey's questions," he decided.

How can I make a difference?
What can I do for others?
How can I help my community?
What is my purpose?

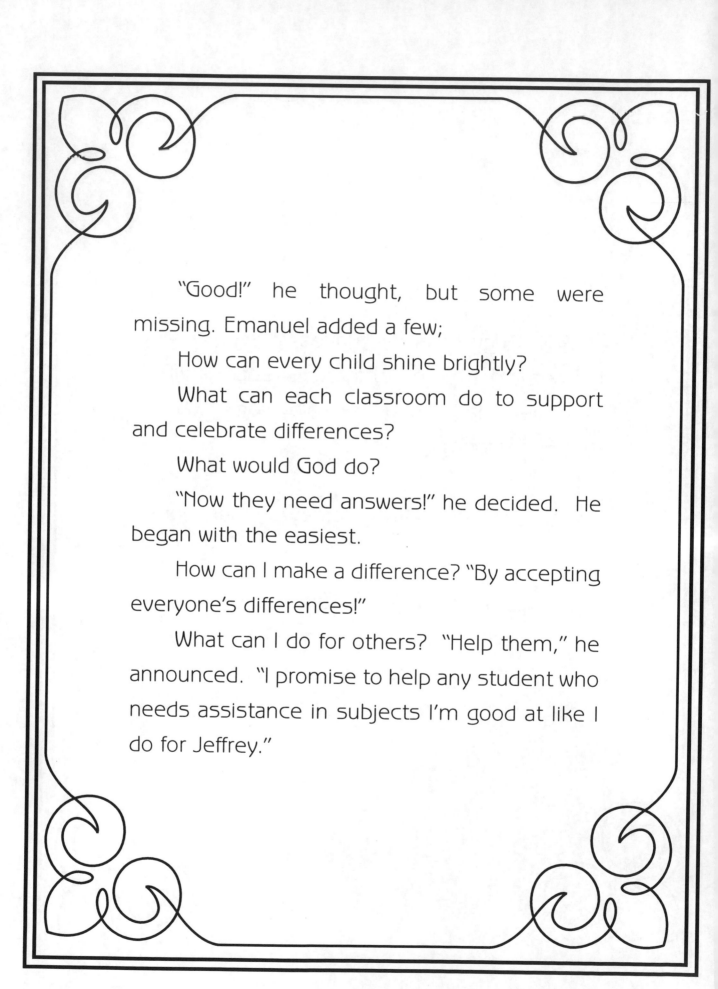

"Good!" he thought, but some were missing. Emanuel added a few;

How can every child shine brightly?

What can each classroom do to support and celebrate differences?

What would God do?

"Now they need answers!" he decided. He began with the easiest.

How can I make a difference? "By accepting everyone's differences!"

What can I do for others? "Help them," he announced. "I promise to help any student who needs assistance in subjects I'm good at like I do for Jeffrey."

How can I help my community? "I can encourage others to do the same!"

What is my purpose? "To help Jeffrey!" he proclaimed, "and let him shine!"

How can every child shine brightly? "With someone who believes in them." he continued, "like teachers and classmates who recognize an individual's strengths and base their achievements from there."

What can each classroom do to support and celebrate differences? "Become a team!" he shouted, "with players who combine their strengths to achieve victory!"

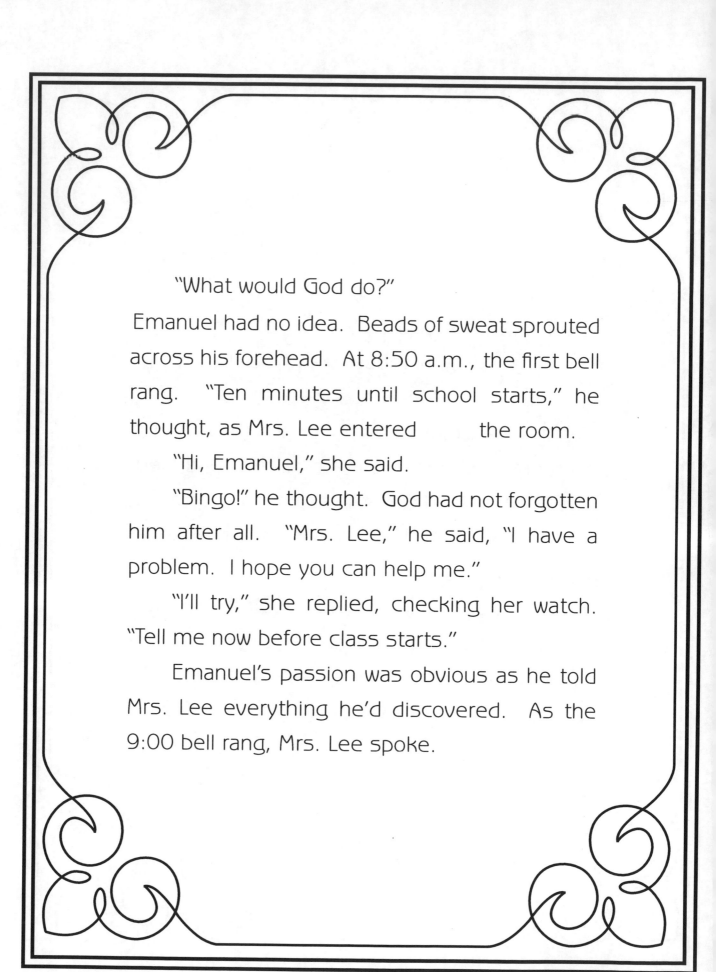

"What would God do?"

Emanuel had no idea. Beads of sweat sprouted across his forehead. At 8:50 a.m., the first bell rang. "Ten minutes until school starts," he thought, as Mrs. Lee entered   the room.

"Hi, Emanuel," she said.

"Bingo!" he thought. God had not forgotten him after all. "Mrs. Lee," he said, "I have a problem. I hope you can help me."

"I'll try," she replied, checking her watch. "Tell me now before class starts."

Emanuel's passion was obvious as he told Mrs. Lee everything he'd discovered. As the 9:00 bell rang, Mrs. Lee spoke.

DRAGONFLY

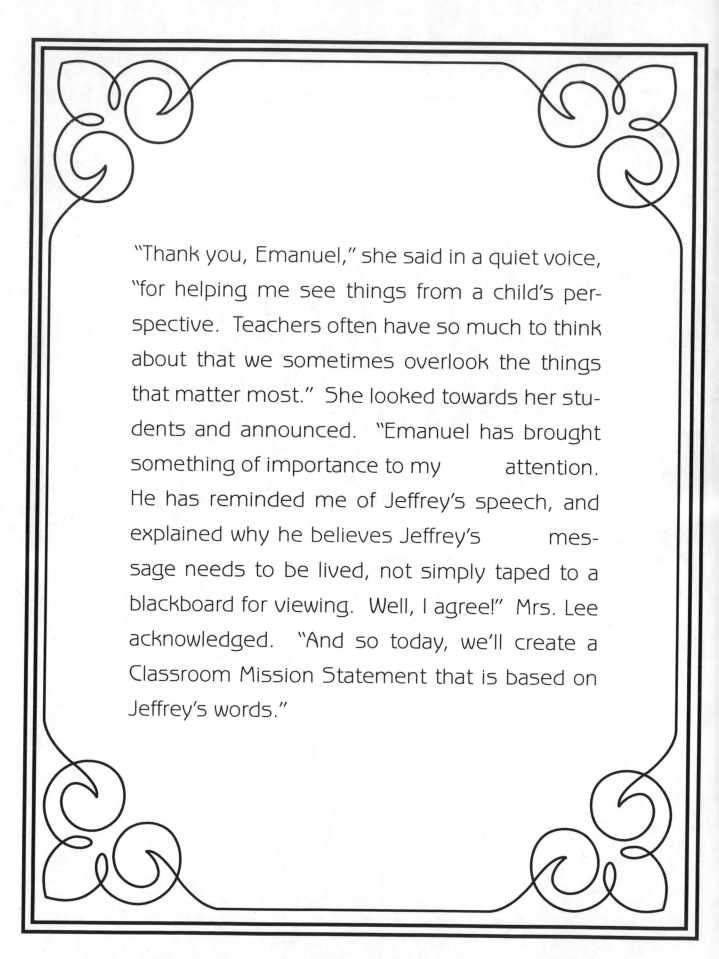

"Thank you, Emanuel," she said in a quiet voice, "for helping me see things from a child's perspective. Teachers often have so much to think about that we sometimes overlook the things that matter most." She looked towards her students and announced. "Emanuel has brought something of importance to my   attention. He has reminded me of Jeffrey's speech, and explained why he believes Jeffrey's   message needs to be lived, not simply taped to a blackboard for viewing. Well, I agree!" Mrs. Lee acknowledged. "And so today, we'll create a Classroom Mission Statement that is based on Jeffrey's words."

Then she whispered to Emanuel. "You truly are my little angel, aren't you?"

Emanuel's heart raced. "Thanks for the compliment, Mrs. Lee, but Jeffrey's the angel who wrote these words, remember?" He turned and faced Jeffrey, cleared his throat and spoke to the class:

"As my best friend said, 'If we put our gifts together, we too...could be powerful!' He's the wisest person I know."

Emanuel smiled as a beam of sunlight fell on Jeffrey's desk. Everyone clapped and clapped. Jeffrey sat up straight and truly listened. It was his turn to SHINE.

Personal Conscience Character

The Power of One

My Perspective of God

Self Portrait: In Heaven

My Life's Purpose

Confidence Shield

Wish List